BENCHED
DEALING WITH SPORTS INJURIES

WHAT IF I BREAK A TOOTH?

Gareth Stevens
PUBLISHING

BY SARAH MACHAJEWSKI

Please visit our website, www.garethstevens.com. For a free color catalog of all our high-quality books, call toll free 1-800-542-2595 or fax 1-877-542-2596.

Library of Congress Cataloging-in-Publication Data

Names: Machajewski, Sarah, author.
Title: What if I break a tooth? / Sarah Machajewski.
Description: New York : Gareth Stevens Publishing, [2017] | Series: Benched: dealing with sports injuries | Includes bibliographical references and index.
Identifiers: LCCN 2016005383 | ISBN 9781482448924 (pbk.) | ISBN 9781482448863 (library bound) | ISBN 9781482448399 (6 pack)
Subjects: LCSH: Sports injuries–Juvenile literature. | Sports accidents–Juvenile literature. | Teeth–Wounds and injuries–Juvenile literature.
Classification: LCC RD97 .M33 2017 | DDC 617.1/027–dc23
LC record available at http://lccn.loc.gov/2016005383

First Edition

Published in 2017 by
Gareth Stevens Publishing
111 East 14th Street, Suite 349
New York, NY 10003

Designer: Katelyn E. Reynolds
Editor: Ryan Nagelhout

Photo credits: Cover, p. 1 (background photo) Brian Paulson/Shutterstock.com; cover, p. 1 (girl) Val Thoermer/Shutterstock.com; cover, pp. 1–24 (background texture) mexrix/Shutterstock.com; cover, pp. 1–24 (chalk elements) Aleks Melnik/Shutterstock.com; p. 5 Patrick Foto/Shutterstock.com; p. 7 Hatchapong Palurtchaivong/Shutterstock.com; p. 9 andrey oleynik/Shutterstock.com; p. 11 Paolo Bona/Shutterstock.com; p. 13 Suzanne Tucker/Shutterstock.com; p. 15 ntstudio/Shutterstock.com; p. 17 wavebreakmedia/Shutterstock.com; p. 19 John Giustina/Photographer's Choice/Getty Images; p. 21 Ian Horrocks/Newcastle United via Getty Images.

Printed in the United States of America

CPSIA compliance information: Batch #CS16GS : For further information contact Gareth Stevens, New York, New York at 1-800-542-2595

CONTENTS

 Words in the glossary appear in **bold** type the first time they are used in the text.

A BREAK
TO THE FACE

Whether you're out on the field, on the ice, or even on the monkey bars, it's fun to be active. But it's important to be safe, too. **Injuries** can happen at any time, but kids who play sports are more likely to get hurt.

Cuts, bumps, and breaks are common sports injuries. One kind of break can happen right under your nose—to your teeth! Your teeth are a central part of your face, so your chance of injuring them is greater than that of injuring other parts. What happens if you hurt a tooth?

✗ THE GAME PLAN

1. Your teeth are in one of your most important body parts—your head! Your head also holds your brain, eyes, nose, and mouth. It needs to be **protected**!

Your teeth are used for smiling, talking, and chewing. You would do all those things a bit differently if you were missing teeth.

STUDYING THE STATS

Athletes are people who play sports. They know that injuries are often a part of the game. According to a 2013 study, athletes have a 10 **percent** chance of injuring their face or teeth each season.

Each year, about 15 million Americans suffer **dental** injuries. These injuries take many forms. Your teeth can crack, break, and split. They can be jammed into your gums or get knocked out completely. It's thought that about 5 million teeth are lost each year due to sports.

1. Over a career, athletes have about a 45 percent chance of getting a dental injury. That covers almost half of all the time they spend playing.

Studies have shown that sports-related injuries account for between 13 and 39 percent of all dental injuries.

WHAT'S IN A TOOTH?

Take a look at your teeth. The part you can see is called the crown. The crown is covered with a hard **tissue** called enamel. It protects the blood supply and **nerve** endings inside the tooth.

Every tooth has a root, which you usually can't see. It's hidden within the gums. The root is attached to your jaw, keeping the tooth in place. Our teeth are very strong, even stronger than bone! Imagine how much force is needed to break them.

✕ THE GAME PLAN

People have two sets of teeth—baby teeth and adult teeth. Baby teeth fall out, but adult teeth should stay with us for life. It's important to take care of them.

Enamel is the hardest tissue in our body. It protects our teeth, but even enamel can't stand up to some sports injuries.

enamel

gum

crown

neck

root

jawbone

nerve

blood supply

RISKY SPORTS

Our teeth are very strong, but sports are often tougher. It's no surprise most dental injuries are sports related. Your teeth are a central part of your face, which can be at the center of the action. But some sports are more dangerous, or not safe, for your teeth than others.

Baseball and basketball have the highest number of players who get their teeth knocked out. Hockey, soccer, and rugby are up there, too. However, injuries happen in every sport. Dentists say any kid playing a sport should wear a mouth guard, just to be safe.

In general, contact sports have the highest number of injuries. A contact sport is a sport in which players come into contact with, or touch, each other or objects. When elbows, heads, knees, and legs come into contact, teeth sometimes get caught in the mix.

HIGH-CONTACT SPORTS

acrobatics	handball	skydiving
basketball	ice hockey	soccer
bicycling	in-line skating	softball
boxing	lacrosse	squash
equestrian events	martial arts	surfing
extreme sports	racquetball	volleyball
field events	rugby	water polo
field hockey	shot putting	weight lifting
football	skateboarding	wrestling
gymnastics	skiing	

KINDS OF INJURIES

There are four main kinds of dental injuries. A crown fracture is a break to the white part of the tooth. A tooth can be jammed or pushed into the gums. It can also be loosened in its **socket**. Finally, a tooth can be completely knocked out.

In general, great force is needed to injure a tooth. The force could come from a flying ball or puck. It could be another player's elbow, head, or knee. You could fall and hit your teeth against a hard surface. In sports, anything can happen!

✕ THE GAME PLAN

Crown fractures are the most common dental injury. This injury can really hurt if the inside of the tooth, the pulp, is **exposed**. A tiny chip or crack, however, might not hurt at all. But it might look a bit funny.

✕ — DENTAL INJURIES — ✕

✕ crown fracture
(a break, chip, or split in the white part of the tooth)

✕ tooth intrusion
(tooth is pushed into the gums)

✕ tooth extrusion
(tooth is knocked loose in its socket)

✕ tooth avulsion
(tooth is knocked out)

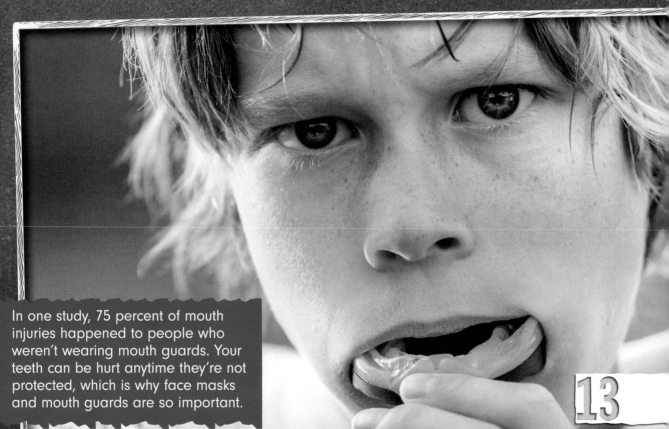

In one study, 75 percent of mouth injuries happened to people who weren't wearing mouth guards. Your teeth can be hurt anytime they're not protected, which is why face masks and mouth guards are so important.

13

OUCH!
NOW WHAT?

Let's say you took an elbow to the face during soccer. Or maybe you flipped over the handlebars of your bike. If you've broken a tooth, you'll probably know right away.

Look in the mirror or have an adult look at your teeth. Check to see if they're still there. Does a tooth look chipped, cracked, or broken? Try wiggling it with your tongue to see how it feels. Most importantly, does it hurt? If it does, you need to go to the dentist.

✕ THE GAME PLAN

1. If you've broken or knocked out a tooth, try to keep the piece (or pieces) you can find. Handle the tooth gently. Keep it in a glass of milk until you get to the dentist. The milk keeps the tooth wet and its roots alive while it's out of your mouth!

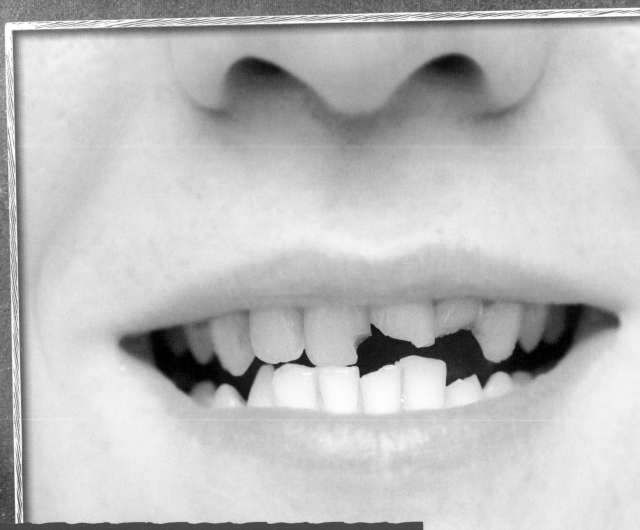

Broken or hurt teeth need to be treated as soon as possible. Teeth have a blood supply, nerves, and tissues that can actually die as time passes. The sooner you get to the dentist, the better.

GETTING FIXED UP

It's okay to feel scared if you break a tooth. It's also okay to feel scared about going to the dentist. Just remember that the dentist is there to help you get better.

The first thing the dentist will do is look at your mouth. Next, they'll take X rays, which are pictures that allow them to see inside the tooth. The dentist will also check to see if the root is broken. Dentists have a lot of **procedures** for fixing broken teeth. In many cases, your tooth can be saved!

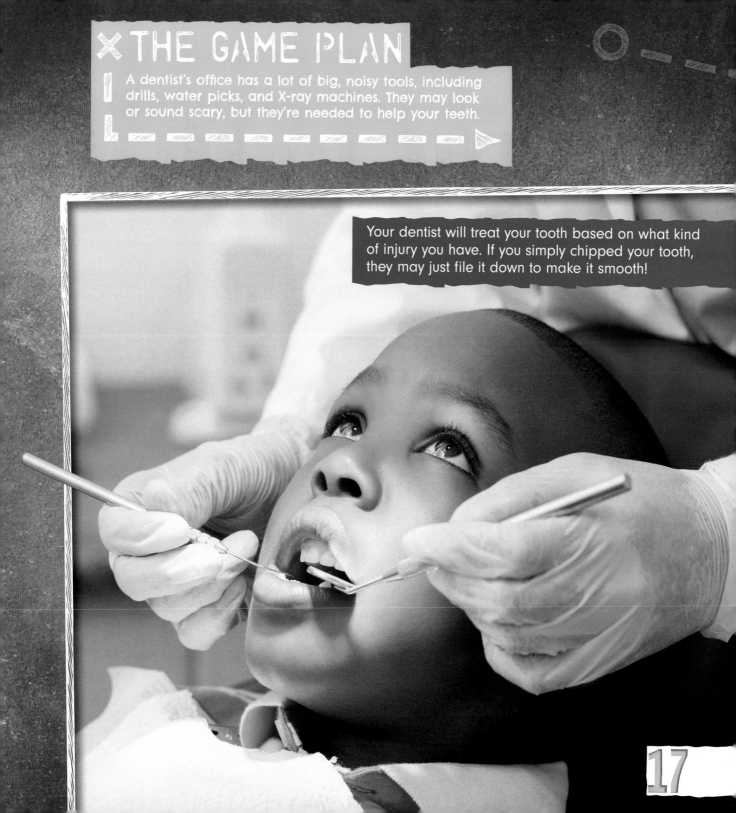

✗ THE GAME PLAN

1 A dentist's office has a lot of big, noisy tools, including drills, water picks, and X-ray machines. They may look or sound scary, but they're needed to help your teeth.

Your dentist will treat your tooth based on what kind of injury you have. If you simply chipped your tooth, they may just file it down to make it smooth!

17

BACK IN THE GAME!

Your **recovery** depends on the kind of break you had. In general, you can get back to playing once your tooth is fixed. However, you might need to rest if your mouth feels sore. And if your tooth still hurts, tell your dentist right away.

Even if you feel fine, you must be careful going forward. Wear a mouth guard anytime you're playing sports. Watch out for people and objects around you. These simple habits will keep you—and your teeth—from getting hurt.

Wearing a mouth guard is the best way to protect your teeth.

A BAD BREAK

English soccer player Peter Crouch knows the pain of dental injuries all too well. In 2013, the Stoke City player ran into Fabricio Coloccini, a Newcastle defender. Coloccini's arm hit Crouch in the face. When he looked down, Crouch saw two of his teeth in his hand! Two more teeth were jammed into his gums.

Crouch was treated by a dentist and later had an operation. "My teeth came out in my hand! Thankfully there was a dentist in the crowd," Crouch said. "He saved them."

✗ THE GAME PLAN

Crouch had to wear a mouth guard and a brace after his operation. He missed a game, but played again a week later.

An athletic trainer rushes to help Crouch, who's holding his teeth in his hand!

GLOSSARY

dental: having to do with teeth

exposed: made able to be seen, especially by being uncovered

injury: hurt or harm

nerve: a part of the body that sends messages between the brain and the rest of the body

percent: part of a whole, measured in parts out of a hundred

procedure: an operation

protect: to keep safe

recovery: the time spent returning to health

socket: a hollow area that something can fit into

tissue: matter that forms the parts of living things

FOR MORE INFORMATION

BOOKS

Herrington, Lisa M. *I Lost a Tooth*. New York, NY: Children's Press, 2015.

Marlowe, Christie. *Sports*. Broomall, PA: Mason Crest, 2015.

WEBSITES

Going to the Dentist
kidshealth.org/kid/feel_better/people/go_dentist.html
This resource walks you through what to expect when you go to the dentist.

Your Teeth
kidshealth.org/kid/htbw/teeth.html
Learn more about your teeth and how to keep them healthy.

INDEX